Learning Sight Words

Vol. 2

Dolch-based reproducible lessons and activities designed to make language acquisition easy and fun.

by Barbara Rankie

ISBN: 978-1-55386-099-0

Acknowledgements

Author – Barbara Rankie

Cover Design – Campbell Creative Services

Editors – Andrew Gaiero, Sara Jordan

Illustrations – Various Contributors

Interior Layout – Darryl Taylor

For further information contact:

Jordan Music Productions Inc.
M.P.O. Box 490
Niagara Falls, NY
U.S.A. 14302-0490

Jordan Music Productions Inc.
Station M, Box 160
Toronto, Ontario
Canada, M6S 4T3

Telephone: 1-800-567-7733
Web Site: www.SongsThatTeach.com
E-mail: sjordan@sara-jordan.com

We acknowledge the financial support of the Government of Canada through the Book Publishing Industry Development Program (BPIDP) for our publishing activities.

Canada

Table of Contents

Tips for the Teacher

We are very proud to present the *Learning Sight Words* series which can be used independently or as a companion resource supplementing the *Singing Sight Words* audio series.

Learning Sight Words is based on the list of 220 frequently used service words compiled by Edward William Dolch, Ph.D., and the related list of 95 high-frequency nouns. Often referred to as high-frequency or sight words, it is estimated that 50-75% of all words used in school books, library books, newspapers and magazines are included in the Dolch Basic Sight Vocabulary.

The lessons in this book all include two teacher-directed activities for the entire class or group, as well as individual activities which the classroom teacher may wish to photocopy for the class.

Each lesson is based on suggested vocabulary from the age and grade-appropriate Dolch word lists. Word cards needed for the teacher-directed activities can be found on our website at: www.SongsThatTeach.com/sightwords.

We are very pleased to have Barbara Rankie author this series. Barbara, who holds a B.A. in Linguistics and Psychology from the University of Ottawa and a B.Ed. from Queens University, has been a teacher with the Niagara District School Board for the past 18 years. She is highly regarded by her peers for the creativity and enthusiasm she infuses into all of her lessons.

Please visit our website, www.SongsThatTeach.com to further enhance classroom learning. You'll find pen pal classes from around the world, contests, cartooning lessons and much more.

Enjoy!

Sara Jordan
President

Suggested Vocabulary List

a	little
all	out
and	play
as	ring
bell	street
bells	that
boy	the
children	them
day	too
down	up
garden	way
girl	well
has	where
hill	you
in	
it	

Group Lesson 1 - Word Outlines

Materials:
- white paper or construction paper
- an "outline" format of words from the suggested vocabulary list

Preparation:
For this activity you will need to print the suggested vocabulary list as well as the same list in an "outline" format found at: www.SongsThatTeach.com/sightwords Print outlines of these same words for later use in this activity.

How it Works:
Choose five words from the vocabulary list. Show the students the list of words you have chosen. Take the first word and outline the shape of the letters with a marker. Cut out the word so that the students can see the shape of the word. Outline the other words, bringing to their attention the height of the letters. Then cut them out. Display the cut-out words on the board or in a pocket chart. Next, show the students the blank outline/ frame of each of the words and also display them. Challenge the students to match the shape of the words to the blank frame and then print the letters in the blank frame to see if they were correct.

Group Lesson 2 - Ring the Bell!

Materials:
- word cards with words from the suggested vocabulary list
- a bell for children to ring

Preparation:
Print out word cards from our website at: www.SongsThatTeach.com/sightwords

How it Works:
Hand out a word card to each student. The teacher says for example, "Anyone who has the word **street**, may come and ring the bell." The student with the word rings the bell and displays the word on the board or in a pocket chart. Say and clap the letters together. This lesson can be varied by calling several words at a time. Continue until all of the students have had a chance to share their words.

Activity 1

Where is the bell? Color the spaces with the words to find out.

Color these words spaces yellow: **bell** and **ring**.

Color these words spaces blue: **boy, it, well, that, little, girl, them, the, up, in** and **has**.

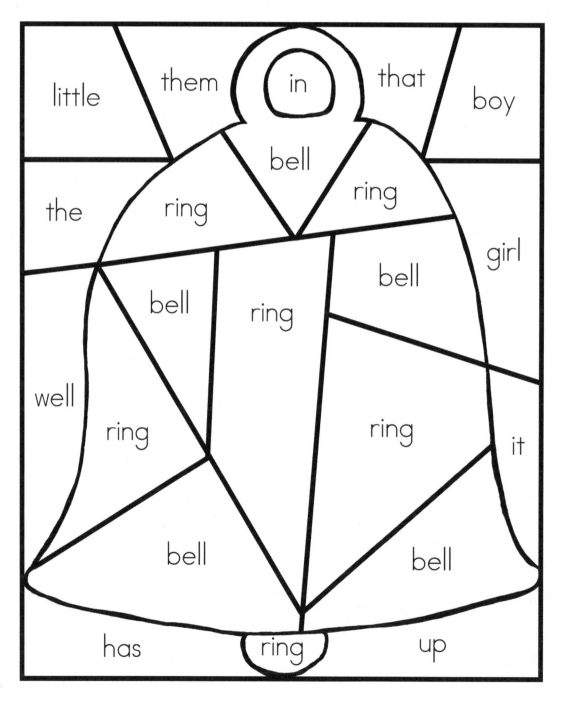

Learning Sight Words, Vol. 2 © 2008 Sara Jordan Publishing

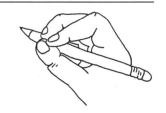

Activity 2

Practice tracing the words below.

hill   down   girl

way   play   you

Complete the sentences using the words above.

Children _____ in the garden.

The _____ plays all day.

The boy plays on the _____ .

_____

Activity 3

Where can you ring the bells? Fill in the blanks using the word bank.

Ring them in the g_____ .

Ring them in the s_____ .

Ring them up and _____ the

_____ . Ring them

everywhere !

Word Bank			
down	garden	hill	street

Learning Sight Words, Vol. 2 © 2008 Sara Jordan Publishing

Group Lesson 1 - What Am I?

Materials: • word cards for: dog, cat, cow, pig, fly, bear and rabbit

Preparation: Print out word cards from our website at: www.SongsThatTeach.com/sightwords

How it Works:
Review the animal words with students before you begin the game. Pin the animal cards on the backs of some students and have them stand in front of the group. The students need to figure out which animal card is pinned on them by asking questions of the group. e.g., "Do I hop?" "Am I a bug?" Each student gets a turn to ask one question and to make one guess. When each student has had a chance, give the students a second turn. The game continues this way until the rest of the class is able to guess who they are.

Suggested Vocabulary List

a	just
after	let
away	my
back	not
bear	now
big	of
cat	on
come	out
cow	pig
do	please
dog	rabbit
fly	ran
get	run
go	said
had	say
have	stop
her	that
here	there
his	too
I	way
is	what
it	

Group Lesson 2 - Complete the Sentence

Materials:
• sentence strips (one for each student)
• word cards with words from the suggested vocabulary list
• crayons and paper for each student

Preparation: Prepare sentence strips with words used in this chapter. Some examples: A _____ ran after the _____. A cow ran _____. Please rabbit _____ back.
Prepare enough sentences so that each student can take one sentence strip.

How it Works:
Place the sentence strips in a pocket chart and have students choose words to complete the sentences. Read the sentences together to make sure that the words they have chosen make sense. Once all of the sentences have been completed, give each student a sentence strip on which they will print the missing word and then illustrate the sentence. The sentences may also be made into a pattern book or story to be put together as a class Big Book.

Activity 1

Name each animal with the help of the word bank.

_____

- - - - - - - - - - -

_____

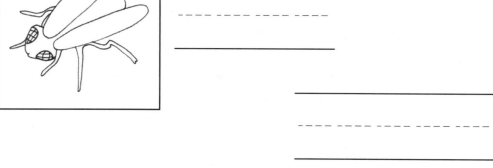

Word Bank					
bear	cat	dog	fly	pig	rabbit

Learning Sight Words, Vol. 2 © 2008 Sara Jordan Publishing

Activity 2

Complete the story about my dog. Use the words in the word bank.

I have a _____ .

It _____ after my rabbit.

I say, "Stop. _____ here."

_____ dog runs _____ .

I _____ to run after her.

_____ a dog!

Word Bank						
away	Come	dog	have	My	runs	What

Activity 3

What is it? Complete the sentences so that they match the pictures.

That _____ a pig.
(is) / (is not)

That _____ a cow.
(is) / (is not)

That _____ a fly.
(is) / (is not)

That _____ a bear.
(is) / (is not)

That _____ a rabbit.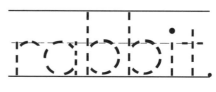
(is) / (is not)

Learning Sight Words, Vol. 2 © 2008 Sara Jordan Publishing

Group Lesson 1 - Direction Words

Materials:
- word cards with words from the suggested vocabulary list
- an object like a chair or a bench

Preparation: Print out word cards from our website at: www.SongsThatTeach.com/sightwords including direction words (**over**, **under**, **up**, **down**, **in** and **out**) on different colored paper.

Suggested Vocabulary List

a	out
after	over
all	play
and	rain
are	robin
bed	round
bird	school
can	see
come	that
comes	the
day	to
down	under
fly	up
giving	water
go	we
ground	
head	
I	
in	
is	
kitty	
little	
look	
my	
of	

How it Works:
Place the direction words in a pile, face down. Give each student a word card. Draw a direction card and have students identify the word. Call out a word and have the child who is holding the word follow the direction word. For example, if the direction word **under** is drawn, say, "I'm looking for the word card **bird**". The student with the word card **bird** crawls under the bench and displays the word card on the board or in the pocket chart. The game continues until all word cards have been called and the direction word followed.

Group Lesson 2 - Rhyming Words

Materials:
- rhyming word cards with words from the suggested vocabulary list

Preparation: Create word cards with the words: **day**, **play**, **fly**, **my**, **I**, **round**, **ground**, **head** and **bed**.

How it Works:
Display the words randomly on the board or in a pocket chart. Review the words by saying, "I'm looking for the word **play**. I like to **play** outside." Have a student identify the word and have all the students chant and clap the letters in the word. Continue this way with the words **my**, **round** and **bed**. Next choose rhyming words and say, "I'm looking for the word **day**. What a nice **day** it is today." Have students identify the word and ask them to look for a word that rhymes with **day**. Place the two words, **play** and **day** together. Continue until the rhyming words have been paired.

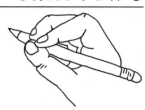

Activity 1

Trace the words.

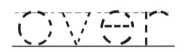 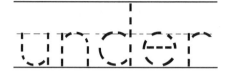

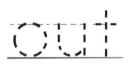  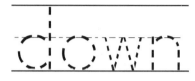

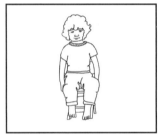

on

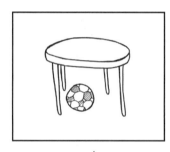 

under

 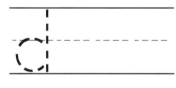

down

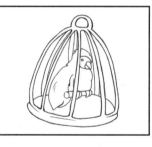 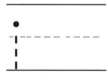

in

 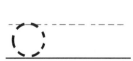

out

over

CHAPTER 3

Activity 2

Follow the word "fly". Color it blue to help the robin to find the worm.

head	giving	fly	fly	fly
that	school	robin	play	fly
water	fly	fly	fly	fly
round	fly	rain	comes	head
fly	fly	see	all	bed
fly	my	we	look	can
fly	fly	worm	ground	day

Activity 3

Complete the poem using the words from the word bank.

See the b_____ fly

round and _____ .

All the way down

to the _____ .

In the w_____

it can _____

after a very rainy _____ .

Word Bank
bird
day
ground
play
round
water

Learning Sight Words, Vol. 2 © 2008 Sara Jordan Publishing

Suggested Vocabulary List

and	that
ask	this
can	water
cat	what
could	you
do	
fish	
for	
give	
I	
is	
it	
know	
may	
me	
milk	
my	
no	
not	
of	
please	
some	

Group Lesson 1 - Word Game

Materials:
- paper body parts of a cat that can be assembled (head, body, tail, four legs, ears, whiskers, etc.)
- paper or chalkboard

Preparation: Make a cat that can be assembled.

How it Works:

The game is played like "Hangman" but you build a cat when the letters are guessed incorrectly. The game begins by choosing a word from the suggested vocabulary list. Make the same number of lines as there are letters in the word (ie. for the word **please** show _ _ _ _ _ _). Have students take turns naming a letter that they think will be in the word. If the letter they choose is in the word, write the letter in the appropriate space. If the letter they choose is not part of the word, begin building the cat. The students try to guess what the word is before the cat is built. Variations of the game would be to have one team play against the other, boys against girls or to have students play in pairs.

Group Lesson 2 - Pass the Bag

Materials:
- word cards with words from the suggested vocabulary list
- a bag
- music

Preparation: Print out word cards from our website at: www.SongsThatTeach.com/sightwords

How it Works:

Students sit in a circle. Place the words in a bag. Start the music and have the students pass the bag. When the music stops, a student reaches in, pulls out a word and reads it to the class. Have the students chant the letters in the word and then place it on the board.

Activity 1

Color the fish with these words red: **could**, **of** and **may**.

Color the fish with these words yellow: **please**, **some** and **ask**.

Color the fish with these words brown: **what**, **if** and **know**.

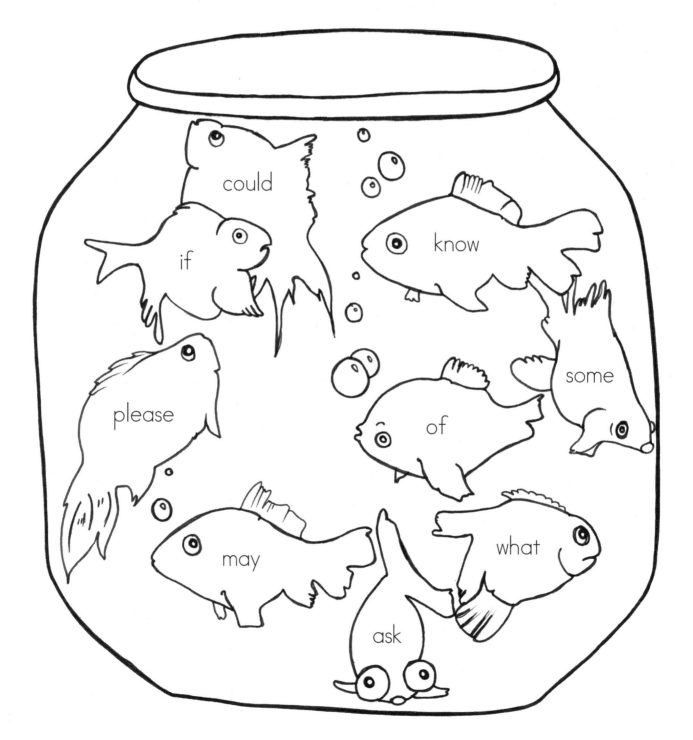

Learning Sight Words, Vol. 2 © 2008 Sara Jordan Publishing

Activity 2

Do you know what this is?

Word Bank			
fish	milk	cat	water

This is a f_____.

That is my m_____.

This is a c_____.

That is a f_____ in w_____.

Activity 3

Complete the sentences using the words in the word bank.

1. May I _____ you water?

2. _____ I do that for you?

3. _____ give me milk.

4. Do you _____ my cat?

5. _____ can I give you?

Word Bank				
Can	give	know	Please	What

Learning Sight Words, Vol. 2 © 2008 Sara Jordan Publishing

Group Lesson 1 - Read for Money

Materials:
- word cards with words from the suggested vocabulary list
- play money

Preparation: Print out word cards from our website at:
www.SongsThatTeach.com/sightwords

How it Works:
Create two equal teams. Choose two students, one from each team.
Hold up a word card. The first student to identify the word gets play money.
The game continues in this way with each person on the team taking a turn.
The team with the most amount of money is the winner.

Group Lesson 2 - Cheer Your Word

Materials:
- two sets of word cards with words from the suggested vocabulary list

Preparation: Print out word cards from our website at:
www.SongsThatTeach.com/sightwords

How it Works:
Give each student a word card. Place the other set of cards in a container.
Choose a word from the container and read it aloud. The student who has
the card stands up, reads the word and leads the cheering of the
letters. If the word is "floor", the student will start by saying, "Give me an F."
The other students will respond by cheering, "F". Continue until all the letters
have been cheered.

Suggested Vocabulary List

a	me
all	money
and	new
at	of
ball	on
blue	one
boat	out
box	play
can	red
car	ring
coat	take
do	that
doll	the
floor	think
for	three
four	two
funny	we
game	what
have	with
horse	yellow
house	yes
I	you
is	
it	
like	
look	

Group Lesson 3 - Reading Board Game

yes	of	money	all	take	house
floor					ball
what					funny
think					look
horse					with
like					game
start	doll	that	play	you	we

Game Instructions

1. Put playing pieces on "start".
2. Each player takes a turn rolling the die and moving the number of spaces.
3. When a player lands on a square, he/she reads the word.
4. If the player reads the word correctly, he/she takes a token (play money, counters, etc.)
5. First person to collect ten tokens wins the game.

Learning Sight Words, Vol. 2 © 2008 Sara Jordan Publishing

Activity 1

Print the words next to the pictures. Print the "number word" first and then the "object". Color each picture.

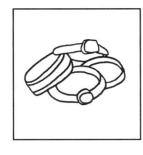 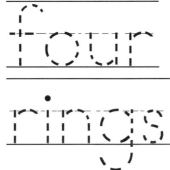

four
rings

 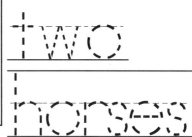

two
horses

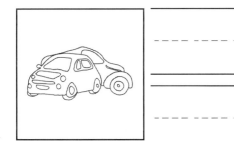

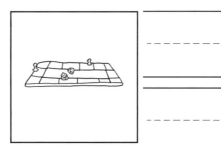

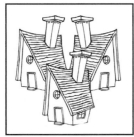

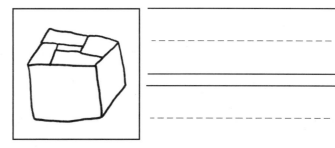

Word Bank									
box	cars	four	game	horses	houses	one	rings	three	two

Activity 2

Use the words to complete.

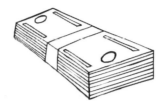

I have money for:

____ _____ _____
a y_____ _____ .

coat

____ _____ _____
a b_____ _____ .

boat

____ _____ _____
a n_____ _____ .

doll

____ _____ _____
a r_____ _____ .

ball

Word Bank			
red	new	blue	yellow

Learning Sight Words, Vol. 2 © 2008 Sara Jordan Publishing

Group Lesson 1 - Bag of Letters

Materials:
- letters used to spell the words from the vocabulary list
- small plastic bags, one for each child
- word cards with words from the suggested vocabulary list
- pocket chart to display words

Preparation:
Print out word cards from our website at:
www.SongsThatTeach.com/sightwords
Sort the letters of each of the words into the small plastic bags so that each bag makes a word. Place the word cards in a pocket chart.

How it Works:
Demonstrate the activity in a large group first. With the students, read over the list of words that will be made once the children arrange the letters from their bags. Take a bag and place the letters in the pocket chart. Have the students rearrange the letters to make one of the words on the list. Next, give each student a plastic bag with letters. Once the students have rearranged their letters to make a word, they find the word in the pocket chart that matches it. The student takes the card out of the pocket chart to match to their word.

Suggested Vocabulary List

a	me
all	men
are	my
at	not
came	one
did	open
do	please
door	run
for	said
four	say
give	see
good-bye	take
good-day	they
had	three
hand	to
have	too
here	two
him	we
house	well
how	were
I	what
in	you
it	
man	

Group Lesson 2 - Word Similarities

Materials:
- word cards with words from the suggested vocabulary list, that begin with the same letter

Preparation:
Print out word cards from our website at:
www.SongsThatTeach.com/sightwords

How it Works:
Give a word card to each student. Explain to the students that they will be sorting themselves into groups with words that begin with the same letter. When they are given a signal, students sort themselves into groups. Once in their groups, students share their words aloud with the other students in the group. Continue the game using other criteria (ie. words that end in the same letter or have a certain vowel in them).

Activity 1

Complete the sentences using the words **for**, **four**, **to** and **too**. One word will be used twice.

1. We run _____ the house.

2. Open the door _____ me.

3. The _____ men came to my house.

4. I have a house _____ .

5. It is time _____ lunch.

Word Bank			
for	four	to	too

    Learning Sight Words, Vol. 2 © 2008 Sara Jordan Publishing

Activity 2

Color the squares to find the hidden number.

1. Color these words yellow: **three, they, too, take, to, two**

2. Color these words blue: **him, have, here, hand, had, how**

3. Color these words brown: **one, open, please, run, you**

4. Color these words red: **for, four, door**

5. Color these words black: **good-day, good-bye, give**

good-day	for	give	door	good-bye
how	door	had	four	hand
three	four	door	for	they
open	to	here	four	one
too	have	please	door	take
him	you	two	for	run

Activity 3

Color the doors that have a **long ē**, red.

Color the doors that have a **short ă**, blue.

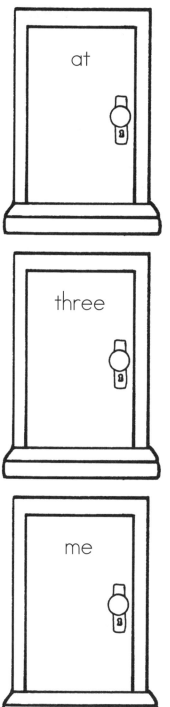

Learning Sight Words, Vol. 2 © 2008 Sara Jordan Publishing

Group Lesson 1 - First Letter Groups

Materials: • words from the vocabulary list and previous lists that begin with the letters in "thank you" (The list below includes words from the list in this chapter and the starred words are from the previous chapters.)

T	H	A	N	K	Y	O	U
Take	Have	After	Not*	Kitty*	You	Out*	Up*
Thank	Help	And	Now*	Know*	Yes	Over*	Under*
That	How	Are	No*		Yellow	Of*	
The	Ask					One*	
Them						On*	
They						Open*	

Preparation: Make word cards and the letters THANK YOU.

How it Works:

Place the letters of the words "thank you" randomly in the pocket chart and tell the students that these letters form an expression. Give each student a word card and tell them to sort themselves into groups by their first letters. The students share their word with others in the group. Have students try to guess what words the letters make. Begin by giving clues by presenting the first letter, last letter, second letter, etc. (as in "Hangman") until they have guessed the expression. One by one have the students place their word under the correct letter and read them together as a class.

Group Lesson 2 - Puzzle Maker

Materials: • 8$^{1/2}$" x 11" paper
• crayons
• scissors

Preparation: Print out word cards from our website at:
www.SongsThatTeach.com/sightwords

How it Works:

Students print a word from the vocabulary list on the paper in large letters. They decorate it and then cut it out to make puzzle pieces.

Suggested Vocabulary List

a	milk
after	please
and	ride
are	say
ask	so
can	some
could	take
day	thank
do	that
every	the
for	them
get	they
go	to
good	want
have	what
help	when
how	you
I	
may	
me	

Activity 1

Write the words in the boxes, then find them in the word search.

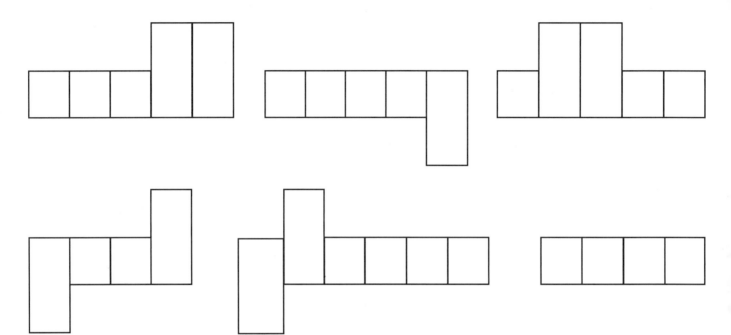

a	f	t	e	r	k	j	p
w	s	p	v	u	x	o	l
c	d	o	e	a	f	i	e
o	i	j	r	h	q	m	a
u	k	c	y	t	e	d	s
l	u	b	n	s	o	m	e
d	m	x	y	v	h	p	b
r	g	o	o	d	r	c	z

Word Bank

after   could   every   good   please   some

Learning Sight Words, Vol. 2 © 2008 Sara Jordan Publishing

Activity 2

Complete the sentences using the correct word.

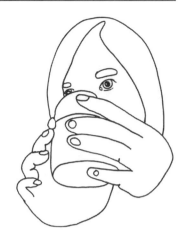

1. I _____ milk, please.

want / what

2. _____ want to help.

Them / They

3. _____ you for the ride.

That / Thank

4. You _____ milk every day.

have / help

5. Please _____ that for me.

go / get

Activity 3

Use **please** and **thank you** in the sentences to show your manners.

When I ask for milk, I say, "May I

have milk , _____ ?"

When you get me milk, I say,

" _____ _____ "

_____ _____ .

When you ask for help, you say,

" _____ help me."

When you get help, you say,

" _____ _____ "

_____ _____ .

    Learning Sight Words, Vol. 2 © 2008 Sara Jordan Publishing

Group Lesson 1 - Pictures and Words

Materials:
- pictures of words from the suggested vocabulary list (nouns– ball, boat, brother, can, car, coat, father, grass, ground, mother, paper, pictures, round, shoe, sister)

How it Works:
Familiarize the students with the words from the vocabulary list. Tell students that some of them will get a picture of an object and others will get a word card. When given the signal, students look for their partner, they stand in a circle and share their word with the rest of the group. Continue the game several times.

Group Lesson 2 - Draw the Sentence

Materials:
- word cards with words in the suggested vocabulary list
- sentence strips
- 12" x 18" sheets of paper for drawing
- crayons

Preparation:
Print out word cards from our website at: www.SongsThatTeach.com/sightwords
Prepare sentence strips with sentences using words from the vocabulary list, one for each student to read and draw.
Examples: A ball is on the grass.
That is my sister's boat.
His father has a coat.
Her brother has a car.

How it Works:
Review words from the vocabulary list. (Use picture cards from Activity 1.) Place the sentence strips in the pocket chart. Give a student a turn to read one of the sentences. After the student has read the sentence, have the whole group repeat it. Continue until all the sentence strips have been read. Each student gets a sentence strip to illustrate.

Suggested Vocabulary List

a	of
all	on
and	paper
ball	picture
boat	round
brother	see
can	shoe
car	sister
coat	that
do	the
father	what
grass	with
ground	you
her	
his	
I	
is	
make	
me	
mother	

Activity 1

Sort the following words into "one syllable" and "two syllable" words:
brother, ground, car, paper, shoe, picture, grass, sister, can, father

<u>two</u> <u>syllables</u>
e.g., mother

brother

<u>one</u> <u>syllable</u>
e.g., you

ground

Learning Sight Words, Vol. 2 © 2008 Sara Jordan Publishing

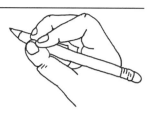

Activity 2

Find the matching rhyming words.

coat
_____

brother
_____

his
_____

ground
_____

me
_____

all
_____

Word Bank

ball	boat	is	mother	round	see

Activity 3

Many people belong in a family: **mother, father, brother, sister, me, you, her.** Find these words and color them red.

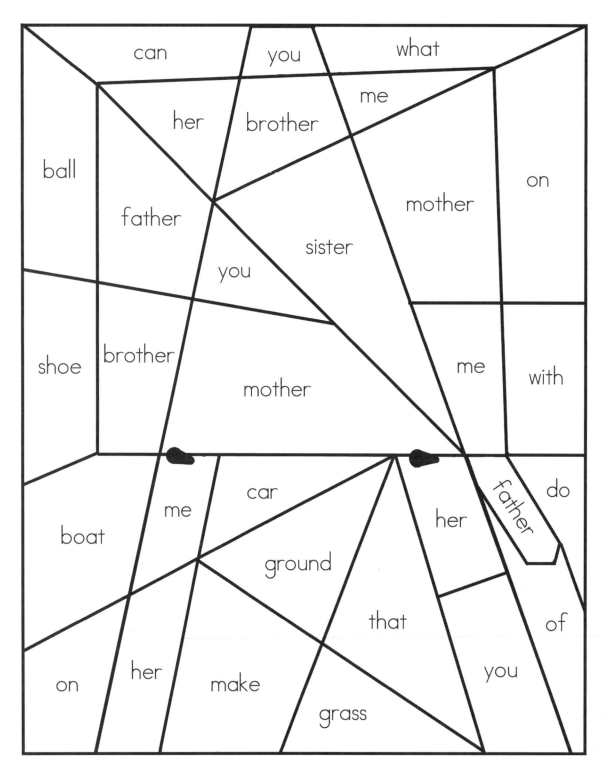

Learning Sight Words, Vol. 2 © 2008 Sara Jordan Publishing

Group Lesson 1 - Draw, Guess and Chant

Materials:
- drawing paper
- crayons
- word cards with words from the suggested vocabulary list that can be drawn (**boat, coat, can, ball,** etc.)

Preparation: Print out word cards from our website at: www.SongsThatTeach.com/sightwords

How it Works:
The object of the game is to have one student from each team draw a picture while his/her teammates try to guess what he/she is drawing.

Divide the students into two teams. Show a word card to one student from each team. Have the students get ready and on the count of three they start drawing the picture for their team. The game ends when one team guesses what the word is. The winning group places the word card in the pocket chart and cheers the letters of the words.

Group Lesson 2 - Similar Words

Materials:
- word cards with rhyming words from the suggested vocabulary list: **boat, coat, all, ball, ground, round, his, is, me, see, mother, brother, shoe, do, you.**

Preparation: Print out word cards from our website at: www.SongsThatTeach.com/sightwords
Randomly place the word cards in a pocket chart.

How it Works:
Read the words in the pocket chart together. Ask students if they hear any words that sound the same and rhyme. Give students turns finding rhyming words and place them side by side in the pocket chart. Once the rhyming words are side by side, have students look for similarities in the spelling patterns.

Suggested Vocabulary List

a	is	what
an	it	with
and	leg	you
are	let	
ask	me	
at	my	
away	not	
back	now	
came	old	
coat	on	
come	once	
did	out	
do	put	
door	said	
duck	say	
floor	shoe	
for	soon	
from	stop	
go	that	
had	the	
he	then	
head	there	
here	to	
his	was	
I	water	
in	went	

Activity 1

Fill in the blanks using words from the word bank.

An old _____ came to my

_____ . He came in. He

had water from his _____ to

his _____ .

He put on a _____ and a

_____ . He went back out the

_____ . There was _____

on the _____ .

Word Bank						
coat	door	floor	head	leg	shoe	water

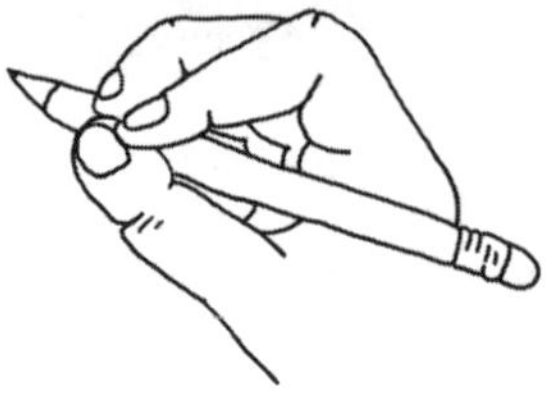

Activity 2

Unscramble the words with the help of the word bank.

_____
- - - - - - - - - - - -
_____

ceno

_____
- - - - - - - - - - - -
_____

ywaa

_____
- - - - - - - - - - - -
_____

otsp

_____
- - - - - - - - - - - -
_____

dsia

_____
- - - - - - - - - - - -
_____

kabc

_____
- - - - - - - - - - - -
_____

ehrte

_____
- - - - - - - - - - - -
_____

own

_____
- - - - - - - - - - - -
_____

rfom

_____
- - - - - - - - - - - -
_____

tup

_____
- - - - - - - - - - - -
_____

oons

Word Bank									
away	back	from	now	once	put	said	soon	stop	there

Learning Sight Words, Vol. 2 © 2008 Sara Jordan Publishing

Suggested Vocabulary List

a	is	you
and	it	
any	just	
as	letter	
ask	little	
away	man	
be	me	
bear	mother	
box	my	
brother	no	
can	not	
cat	of	
could	please	
cow	said	
did	saw	
do	see	
father	sister	
find	song	
for	that	
from	the	
funny	think	
get	to	
go	walk	
have	went	
how	where	
I	who	

Group Lesson 1 - The Envelope Game

Materials:
- envelopes
- word cards with words from the suggested vocabulary list

Preparation: Place words in envelopes. Print out word cards from our website at: www.SongsThatTeach.com/sightwords

How it Works:
Students sit in a circle. While students sing a song (related to mail/writing letters), they pass the envelope with a word inside it. When the song ends, the student who has the envelope takes out the words and shares it with the class. The student leads the cheering of the letters in the word. If the word is **saw**, the student starts by saying, "Give me an S." The others respond. This continues until all the letters have been cheered. A variation would be to have two envelopes moving around the circle at a time.

Group Lesson 2 - Word Completion

Materials:
- letters for words in the suggested vocabulary list
- pocket chart

Preparation: Organize the letters into words.

How it Works:
In a pocket chart, display the letters of the words you have chosen from this chapter leaving off the last letter of each word (ie. ca_, mothe_, thin_, etc.). On display, also have the letters that are needed to complete each word. Students look at the words and try to find the missing letter to complete each one.

Activity 1

Match the words in the word bank to the pictures.

- - - - - - - - - - - - - -

_____

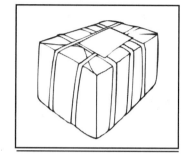

- - - - - - - - - - - - - -

_____

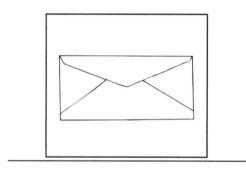

- - - - - - - - - - - - - -

_____

- - - - - - - - - - - - - -

_____

- - - - - - - - - - - - - -

_____

- - - - - - - - - - - - - -

_____

Word Bank
bear   box   cat   cow   letter   song

Learning Sight Words, Vol. 2 © 2008 Sara Jordan Publishing

Activity 2

Color the words on the letters.

Color these words yellow: **walk, think, from.**

Color these words red: **just, please, find, funny.**

Color these words blue: **little, where, father, box.**

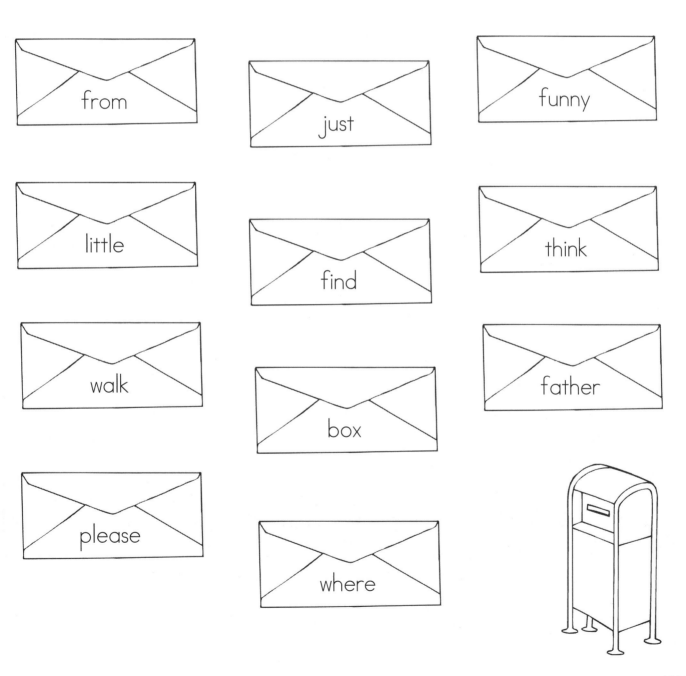

_____
Activity 3

Choose the word that makes sense in each sentence.

The _____ is in the box.
that / cat

Do you _____ the bear?
be / see / me

That is a little _____ .
cow / how

The _____ is funny.
can / man

I want to _____ away.
go / no

Learning Sight Words, Vol. 2 © 2008 Sara Jordan Publishing

Group Lesson 1 - Guessing Game

Materials: • nouns from the suggested vocabulary list (ie. **apple, bird, can, corn,** etc.)

How it Works:

Choose six to eight words from the suggested vocabulary list and display them for the students to see. Review the words first. Explain to the students that you will be giving clues to help them guess what the word is that you are thinking about. (e.g., I am a place where you plant things. What am I?). Continue to give clues until a student has guessed what the word is.

To make the game more difficult, you may give the words to the students and have them think of clues for the other students to guess.

Group Lesson 2 - Spell and Draw

Materials: • word cards (nouns only) with words from the suggested vocabulary list (one for each student)
• crayons
• paper
• scrabble letters (or something similar)

Preparation: Print out word cards from our website at: www.SongsThatTeach.com/sightwords
Provide a small plate with scrabble letters for each student or group of students to use.

How it Works:

Review the words with the students first. Hand-out a word card to each student and have them read it aloud. The students take their word card and form the word using the scrabble letters. They then draw a picture to go with the word.

Suggested Vocabulary List

a	go	we
again	horse	what
all	I	when
an	is	where
and	know	will
apple	look	with
as	me	you
ask	names	
at	new	
away	one	
big	our	
birds	pig	
by	play	
can	pretty	
children	see	
come	sheep	
corn	so	
cow	that	
day	the	
do	them	
farm	then	
fly	there	
from	they	
game	to	
garden	too	
give	want	

Activity 1

Color the words that rhyme with **day**, yellow.

Color the words that rhyme with **there**, red.

Color the words that rhyme with **fly**, blue.

Color the words that rhyme with **pig**, brown.

Color the words that rhyme with **then**, black.

Color the words that rhyme with **game**, green

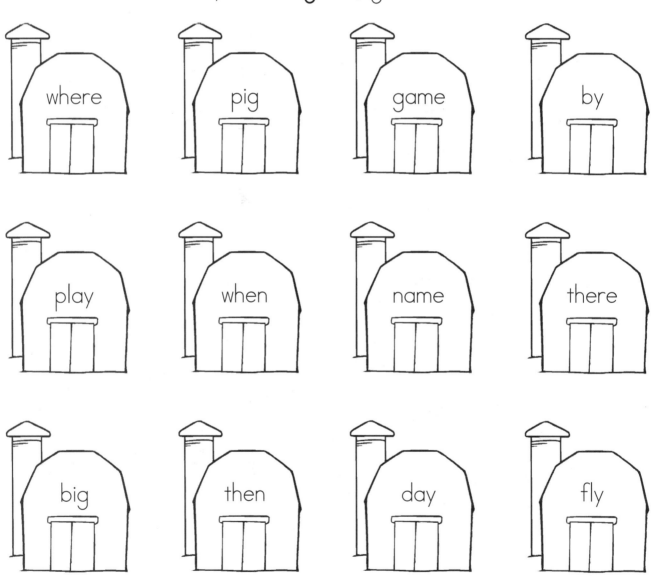

Learning Sight Words, Vol. 2 © 2008 Sara Jordan Publishing

Activity 2

Use the words in the box to complete the sentences.

We will go to the _____.

We will play a new _____.

We will play with a _____.

We will give it an _____.

We can see birds _____.

Word Bank				
fly	game	farm	apple	horse

Activity 3

Use the picture clues to fill in the puzzle.

1.    2.    3.    4.

1. | a | | | | |
2.
3.
4.
5.
6.
7.
8.

5.

6.

7.

8.

Word Bank

sheep   children   garden   birds   apple   horse   corn   farm

Learning Sight Words, Vol. 2 © 2008 Sara Jordan Publishing

CHAPTER 12

Suggested Vocabulary List

a	on
and	over
brother	play
chair	please
come	sister
could	street
day	take
dog	the
down	there
father	they
find	to
have	too
hill	where
house	will
I	with
in	wood
is	yes
it	you
kitty	
like	
little	
live	
me	
mother	
my	
of	

Group Lesson 1 - Family Sentence Strips

Materials:
- sentence strips for each student
- paint
- paper

Preparation: Have materials for painting ready to go.

How it Works:
Discuss all the possible members that could be in a family and how each family is different. Print the names of family members on a chart (father, mother, sister, brother). Also discuss pets that are part of a family and add them to the chart. Show students the sentence strip that they will complete with the sentence starter: I live with my _____. Model for the students how they will complete this sentence to show who is part of their families. Help students complete their sentence strips and then have them paint a picture showing their family.

Group Lesson 2 - The Train Game

Materials:
- word cards with words from the suggested vocabulary list (one for each student)
- container for the word cards

Preparation: Print out word cards from our website at: www.SongsThatTeach.com/sightwords

How it Works:
Review the words you have chosen with the students. Explain to the students that they will be forming a train after each student successfully reads the word that is chosen by the previous student who has joined the train. To start, hold up a word card and ask a student to read the word. This student will be the conductor. The conductor pulls a word card and asks another student to read the word. This student joins the conductor by holding onto his/her shoulders. The second student pulls a card, chooses a student to read the card and play continues until all of the students have become part of the train. For fun, the students can move around the room in train formation until they are back where they started or back at their desks.

Activity 1

Use the words to finish the story.

He lives in a _____ .

It is on this _____ .

It is over the _____ .

He lives with his _____ ,

_____ , _____ and

_____ .

He has a _____ .

Word Bank
mother   hill   brother   house   sister   dog   father   street

Learning Sight Words, Vol. 2 © 2008 Sara Jordan Publishing

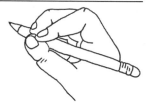

Activity 2

Make new words by changing letters.

1. Change **o** in <u>on</u> to **i**.

2. Change **h** in <u>hill</u> to **w**.

3. Change **v** in <u>live</u> to **k**.

4. Change **e** in <u>me</u> to **y**.

5. Change **br** in <u>brother</u> to **m**.

6. Change **th** in <u>there</u> to **wh**.

Activity 3

Print the missing letters to complete the words. Use the word bank.

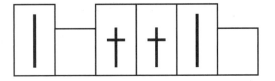

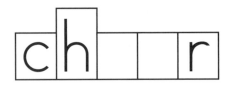

Search for the words.

c	t	h	e	y	m	f	v
o	c	s	w	b	u	d	d
u	x	t	b	p	l	o	o
l	i	t	t	l	e	v	w
d	m	q	i	e	c	e	n
z	r	c	h	a	i	r	y
l	i	v	e	s	v	g	j
x	e	i	c	e	v	m	d

Word Bank

they   please   down   could   over   little   chair   live

Learning Sight Words, Vol. 2 © 2008 Sara Jordan Publishing

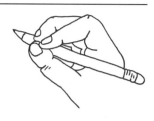

Activity 1

Find the opposites in the word bank.

stop

------ ---- ---- ---- ----

him

------ ---- ---- ---- ----

big

------ ---- ---- ---- ----

boy

------ ---- ---- ---- ----

new

------ ---- ---- ---- ----

over

------ ---- ---- ---- ----

give

------ ---- ---- ---- ----

mother

------ ---- ---- ---- ----

in

------ ---- ---- ---- ----

me

------ ---- ---- ---- ----

up

------ ---- ---- ---- ----

Word Bank	
take	old
little	go
out	her
girl	down
father	you
under	

Activity 2

Find rhyming words and color each set the same color.

now

name

say

take

way

bell

come

how

came

make

game

well

play

some

may

cow

Learning Sight Words, Vol. 2 © 2008 Sara Jordan Publishing

Activity 3

Fill in the crossword with the words in the word bank.

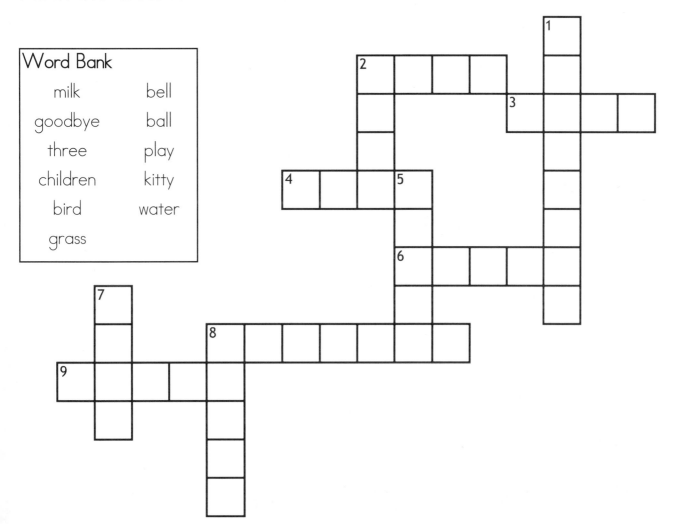

Word Bank

milk	bell
goodbye	ball
three	play
children	kitty
bird	water
grass	

Across

2. It is round.

3. It can fly.

4. It is white.

6. This comes after two.

8. When you go, you say this.

9. A boat needs this.

Down

1. Boys and girls

2. You ring it.

5. A little cat

7. Children do this.

8. A cow likes this.

Activity 4

Unscramble the words. Use the words in the word bank to help you.

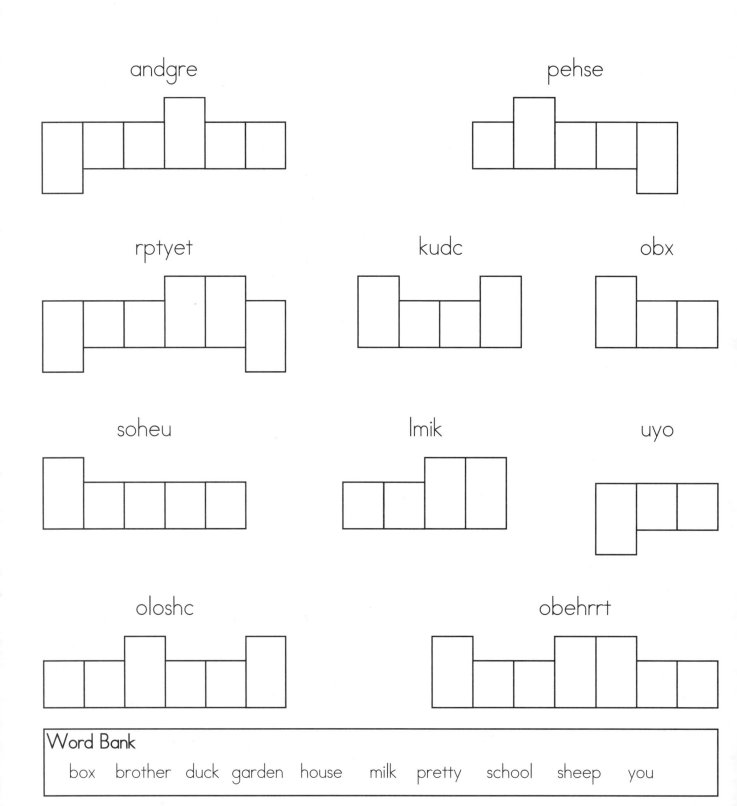

andgre

pehse

rptyet

kudc

obx

soheu

lmik

uyo

oloshc

obehrrt

Word Bank

box   brother   duck   garden   house   milk   pretty   school   sheep   you

Learning Sight Words, Vol. 2 © 2008 Sara Jordan Publishing

Activity 5

There are many things on a farm. Find all of the word bank words in this word search.

```
b  r  o  t  h  e  r  a  t  r  f  e  g  r  a  s  s
a  j  k  p  s  w  p  v  r  a  b  b  i  t  u  x  o
l  q  i  g  z  s  g  a  r  d  e  n  r  n  m  v  m
l  c  t  f  c  h  i  l  d  r  e  n  l  l  d  x  o
p  b  t  a  m  e  e  c  a  t  r  y  i  s  b  a  t
t  e  y  t  j  e  r  s  c  o  r  n  e  f  i  s  h
d  o  g  h  e  p  o  s  z  w  c  a  r  g  r  w  e
m  c  r  e  k  f  b  o  x  d  e  b  c  q  d  k  r
i  e  u  r  n  p  i  g  r  u  y  v  o  i  s  f  i
l  d  v  q  z  l  n  m  e  c  z  q  w  f  p  o  h
k  r  t  h  o  u  s  e  f  k  r  e  n  p  m  l  o
h  i  f  d  v  t  o  b  u  s  s  i  s  t  e  r  r
h  i  l  l  n  l  w  a  t  e  r  g  m  a  n  i  s
k  p  y  b  y  o  h  b  o  y  c  p  r  u  s  o  e
```

Word Bank

boy	children	girl	cat	cow	dog	fly	pig
rabbit	hill	birds	kitty	robin	water	milk	fish
horse	house	ball	box	car	man	men	brother
father	mother	sister	grass	duck	corn	garden	sheep

Chapter 1 – Activity 2
1. Children play in the garden.
2. The girl plays all day.
3. The boys play on the hill.

Chapter 1 – Activity 3
Ring them in the garden.
Ring them in the street.
Ring them up and down the hill. Ring them everywhere!

Chapter 2 – Activity 1
cat   bear
pig   dog
fly   rabbit

Chapter 2 – Activity 2
1. dog
2. runs
3. Come
4. My...runs
5. have
6. What

Chapter 2 – Activity 3
is not
is
is
is not
is not

Chapter 3 – Activity 3
See the bird fly
round and round.
All the way down
to the ground.
In the water
it can play
after a very rainy day.

Chapter 4 – Activity 2
This is a fish.
That is my milk.
This is a cat.
That is a fish in water.

Chapter 4 – Activity 3
1. May I give you water?
2. Can I do the for you?
3. Please give me milk.
4. Do you know my cat?
5. What can I give you?

Chapter 5 – Activity 1
four rings   two horses
two cars   one game
three houses   one box

Chapter 5 – Activity 2
a yellow coat
a blue boat
a new doll
a red ball

Chapter 6 – Activity 1
1. We run to the house.
2. Open the foor for me.
3. The four men came to my house.
4. I have a house too.
5. It is time for lunch.

Chapter 7 – Activity 1
could   every   after
good   please   some

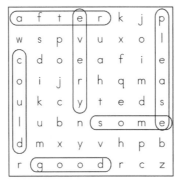

Chapter 7 – Activity 2
1. They
2. want
3. Thank
4. have
5. get

Chapter 7 – Activity 3
When I ask for milk, I say, "May I have milk, please?
When you get me milk, I say, "Thank you."
When you ask for help, you say, "Please help me."
When you get help, you say, "Thank you."

Chapter 8 – Activity 1
two syllables   one syllable
brother   ground
paper   car
picture   shoe
sister   grass
father   can

Chapter 8 – Activity 2
boat
mother
is
round
see
ball

Chapter 9 – Activity 1
An old duck came to my door. He came in. He had water from his head to his leg.
He put on a coat and shoe. He went back out the door. There was water on the floor.

Chapter 9 – Activity 2
once   there
away   now
stop   from
said   put
back   soon

Chapter 10 – Activity 1
cow   box
letter   bear
song   cat

Chapter 10 – Activity 3
The cat is in the box.
Do you see the bear?
That is a little cow.
The man is funny.
I want to go away.

Chapter 11 – Activity 2
farm
game
horse
apple
fly

Learning Sight Words, Vol. 2 © 2008 Sara Jordan Publishing

ANSWER KEYS

Chapter 11 – Activity 3
1. apple
2. farm
3. children
4. horse
5. garden
6. corn
7. sheep
8. birds

Chapter 12 – Activity 1
He lives in a <u>house</u>.
It is on this <u>street</u>.
It is over the <u>hill</u>.
He lives with his <u>mother</u>,
<u>father</u>, <u>sister</u> and
<u>brother</u>.
He has a <u>dog</u>.

Chapter 12 – Activity 2
1. in
2. will
3. like
4. my
5. mother
6. where

Chapter 12 – Activity 3
little   please
chair   they
live   could
        over
        down

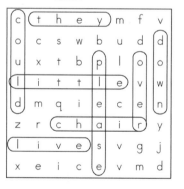

Review – Activity 1
go   her   little
girl   old   under
take   father   out
you   down

Review – Activity 3
Across	Down
2. ball	1. children
3. bird	2. bell
4. milk	5. kitty
6. three	7. play
8. goodbye	8. grass
9. water	

Review – Activity 4
garden   sheep
pretty   duck   box
house   milk   you
school   brother

Review – Activity 5

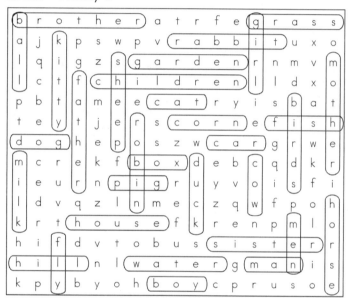

About Sara Jordan Publishing

Sara Jordan Publishing is a recognized leader in the development of high quality, educational materials. Since 1990, the company has been producing educational resources designed to improve literacy, numeracy, language skills (English, French, Spanish and Mandarin), self-esteem, and interest in the world's diverse cultures. These award-winning programs are recommended by teachers and parents and enjoyed worldwide.

Singing Sight Words Series

This comprehensive program, introducing students to over 300 of the most commonly used sight words, has been created for students from K-3 but would be useful for beginning readers of any age. The series is based on the list of 220 frequently used service words compiled by Edward William Dolch, Ph.D., and the related list of 95 high-frequency nouns. The words are presented in order of frequency. It is estimated that 50-75% of all words used in school books, library books, newspapers and magazines are included in the Dolch Basic Sight Vocabulary. The resource books in this series complement the four audio kits by featuring ready-to-use classroom activities, lessons, reproducible worksheets and exercises based on the lessons taught in the songs. Recommended: K-Grade 3

Funky Phonics®: Learn to Read

Blending the best in educational research and practice, Sara Jordan's series, based on Synthetic Phonics, is a structured program providing students with the strategies needed to decode words through rhyming, blending and segmenting. Teachers and parents love the lessons, hands on activities and reproducible worksheets while children find the catchy, toe-tapping tunes fun. The resource books in this series feature ready-to-use classroom activities, lessons, reproducible worksheets and exercises based on the lessons in each of the audio kits. Recommended: K-Grade 2

Bilingual Songs and Bilingual Kids Resource Books

These resources will have your students speaking, singing and laughing in the new language. Each audio book kit covers different subjects ranging from the alphabet, counting, colors, opposites, shapes and sizes to gender, articles, adverbs, punctuation and question words. The accompanying lyrics books may be photocopied by the classroom teacher. Bilingual Kids reproducible resources/activity books include thematic, bilingual, lessons and activities based on the Bilingual Songs series. The activities and lessons are enhanced with cultural references to foreign geography, customs, traditional games, food, and holidays. Available in English-Spanish and English-French formats.

Bilingual Songs: English-Mandarin Chinese, vol. 1

Exciting songs in both English and Mandarin teach the alphabet (English and Pinyin), counting to 10, days of the week, months of the year, weather, seasons, colors, food, Chinese zodiac signs, parts of the body, clothing and family members. Includes reproducible lyrics book in English, Mandarin and Pinyin to aid pronunciation. The singers in English and Mandarin are native speakers. Music accompaniment tracks make singing along karaoke-style fun and class performances a snap.

The Math Unplugged Series

This musical approach to math was created by teachers and is a great alternative to heavier rock and rap programs. It uses an interactive approach. The multiplication and division kits are especially designed to feature and review skip counting in the chorus of every song.

Thematic Songs for Learning Language

Great as an ESL resource! These songs and activities teach common expressions, modes of transportation, clothing, mealtime, weather, parts of the body, pets and rooms of the house. There is even a song teaching the correct use of prepositions!

Character Building Songs

Classroom teachers and music teachers alike will be delighted with this set of songs teaching generosity, responsibility, respect, honesty, etiquette, tolerance, empathy, courage, perseverance and optimism. Separate arrangements allow each song to be sung in unison, as a round or as a classroom performance. The reproducible lyrics book includes lessons and activities.

Lullabies Around the World *Winner of both a Parents' Choice Silver Award and a Directors' Choice Award.* Featuring a dozen singers, each singing in his or her own native tongue. Includes Russian, Polish, Japanese, Mandarin, French, Spanish, Italian, Yiddish, African and American lullabies with their English translations. The accompanying lyrics book (which classroom teachers may reproduce) includes multicultural activities.

Celebrate the Human Race Award-winning songs based on the lives and cultures of children whose homelands boast the Seven Natural Wonders of the World. This is an incredible resource. Each song is musically representative of the culture. Paper dolls and costumes are included in the reproducible lyrics book.

We would like to invite you to join the online community of teachers, parents, friends and associates who receive our electronic newsletter. Every two weeks we faithfully write up teaching ideas, related links and lesson plans based on one, two or even three of our songs. These are all sent, free of charge, along with the free song downloads to recipients of our newsletter.

To subscribe to our English newsletter, visit: www.SongsThatTeach.com.

To subscribe to our Spanish newsletter, visit: www.AprendeCantando.com